FLASH IN THE PAN

RAINCOAST BOOKS

Vancouver

FLASH IN THE PAN

James Barber

with illustrations by the author

Raincoast Books
8680 Cambie Street
Vancouver, B.C.
V6P 6M9
(604) 323-7100

www.raincoast.com

This book was originally published in 1981 by Douglas & McIntyre Ltd.

1 2 3 4 5 6 7 8 9 10

Canadian Cataloguing in Publication Data:

Barber, James, 1923–
Flash in the Pan

Includes index.
ISBN 1-55192-312-2

1. Cookery. I. Title.

TX715.B36 2000   641.5   C00-910016-4

Raincoast Books gratefully acknowledges the support of the Government of Canada, through the Book Publishing Industry Development Program, the Canada Council for the Arts and the Department of Canadian Heritage. We also acknowledge the assistance of the Province of British Columbia, through the British Columbia Arts Council.

Printed and bound in Canada.

es-pecially for Niloufer

the original slow cooker.

Table of Contents

Preface to the New Edition

Way back when, before Martha Stewart, before e-mail, before gourmet websites, when hair was long and money was short, it was the summer of love, a time when everybody wanted to run away and lots of people didn't because they couldn't cook. The Beatles had taught us all how simple music could be, just three chords, so I wrote these books – quick, simple and easy food that made cooking almost as much fun as making love and certainly as easy as strumming a guitar.

The books sold and sold, not just for backpacks but for boats, cottages and bachelor apartments. They never turned up at garage sales; people hung on to them, and I still get regular mail – "Do you still have a spare copy?" – from people who want to give them to their kids but won't part with their own. (An antique book dealer in Victoria recently sold a mint first edition of *Ginger Tea Makes Friends* for $350....) So we reprinted. Even today, all you need to be a good cook is a fry pan and these little books.

James Barber

Introduction

We need a few less cookbooks in the world and a lot more eating books. Kids grow up convinced that there are two kinds of food: company and ordinary. They eat junk food all week and "gourmet" on weekends.

Too often, "gourmet" appears to mean worry, cream, a fistful of money and indigestion. Plus a lot of special ingredients: caviar from Russia, potatoes from Idaho and canned nightingales' tongues from the northeast corner of Berkeley Square. We have forgotten that most cooking in the world is done in a simple pot on top of an even simpler stove, and that people cook three times a day as easily and as naturally as they wake up or go to sleep. Running all over town for ingredients takes time – time we could use to do other things – and more than that, it takes the pleasure out of the end product. Food is not just energy, like gas at the pump; it's a basic pleasure, like sex, and you shouldn't have to have a cookbook open all the time. That's the enduring philosophy behind the flash in the pan.

Chicken and Grapes

There's something elegant about grapes: they're not anything you associate with beer and potato chips. And there's something virtuous about them as you can tell when you take grapes to people in hospital and they're too sick to eat them so you sit and console and one by one they disappear into your mouth. You feel so *good*.

Try sprinkling the inside of a chicken with pepper and salt, then a big teaspoonful of tarragon and the juice of half a lemon. Then poke a bunch of grapes in there. Nothing fussy, just poke them in and cook the chicken in a hot oven (400°F). Baste it occasionally with a little butter, and in an hour you've got something wonderful.

A few grapes for dessert – pull them off the stalks and let them sit in a glass of white wine while you eat the chicken. Or put them unadorned on the table with a bowl of ice water alongside, some slices of lemon sitting it. Washing the grapes at table is one way to get religion without being born again.

To get back to the original recipe – what else do you know that's both elegant and totally foolproof, and takes 15 minutes' preparation at the most?

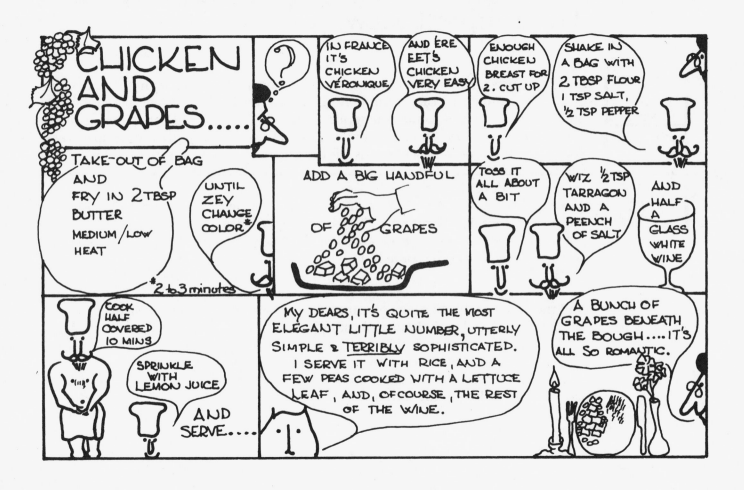

The Simplest Stew

Everybody needs one simple no-work dinner, something that can just quietly get on with itself and cook while you decide: a new job, a new mate, should you move, do the kids really need ballet lessons, and will the office let you keep a moped behind your desk? Too often we make decisions from a position of uncertainty. But if you've got dinner cooking, there is, if not tomorrow, at least an hour ahead of you – an hour containing something predictable.

And then there is this business of using lettuce. Everybody knows lettuce; most of it sits in the bottom of the fridge and gets ancient until it is chucked out. If you cook with it, not only do you get smooth juicy sauces but you also get the satisfaction of knowing that you are not incompetent, unloved and inefficient, because you are saving money and being imaginative. Lettuce is frequently the cheapest vegetable in the market, and it does wonderful things for stews.

Try lining a small pot with lettuce leaves, then putting peas, fresh or frozen, in the little nest you've made. Sprinkle with salt and green dill; put more leaves on top and a tablespoonful of water. Lid on tight, cook about ten minutes. They're like the newest peas you ever tasted.

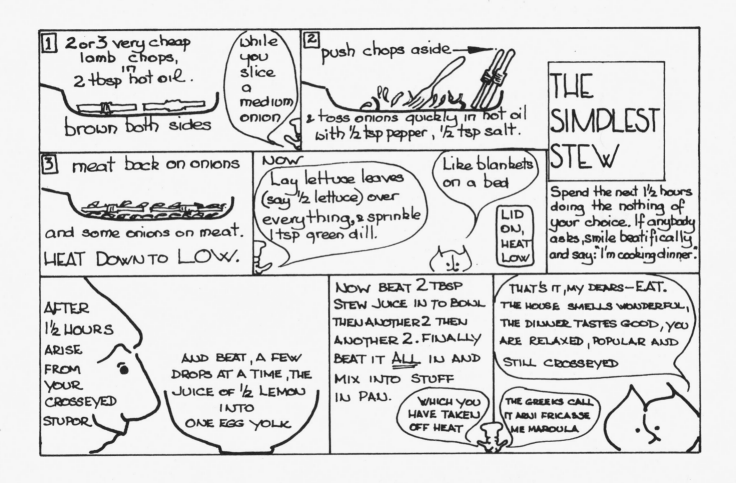

Latkes

Beware of the supermarket pick-up. All those people who used to hang out in discos and prop up the singles bars are now talking gourmet. They lurk in the vegetable section, and talk fancy about zucchini and cold pressed safflower oil; they peer into your shopping basket and come on strong about unsalted butter.

But watch out. All this talk can be learned. Berlitz is now teaching gourmet as an international language to replace Esperanto. There's one sure way to find out if they're bluffing you. Just mention Latkes. There's only one response: "My granma always put a little flour in hers." Anything else is phony, and you should be suspicious.

Of course, if they don't know what latkes are at all, head for the checkout counter immediately. You can't trust nobody these days.

Hot Doughnuts for Breakfast

The early morning zombie's solution to breakfast. Leave the Eggs Benedict to the professionals, don't spoil your lunch with kippers or kedgeree, and don't pretend that porridge is anything more than mush. Take it easy in the mornings – sprinkle a little ground coffee on the burner of your stove, just to perfume the kitchen, and make something simple.

These little doughnuts are the ultimate simplicity, and they are virtually foolproof. In their original version, they were known (quite respectably) as *Pets de Nonne*, which literally translated means Nun's farts. Should you, out of delicacy, prefer the original pre-eighteenth century French, it was *Pets de Pute*, which means Whore's farts.

They are light, airy, delicate and they don't keep.

½ CUP WATER,
1 TSP SUGAR,
4 TBSP BUTTER
⅛ TSP SALT
BRING TO BOIL
AND IMMEDIATELY
TAKE OFF HEAT.

DUMP IN, ALL
AT ONCE, ½ CUP
FLOUR & STIR WELL.
THEN
ONE AT A TIME,
2 EGGS, MIXING
VIGOROUSLY WITH
A FORK. MAKE IT
VERY SMOOTH.

AND COOK,
OVER LOWEST HEAT,
STIRRING UNTIL
IT DOESN'T STICK
TO SIDES

YOU MAY NOT
HAVE TO COOK
IT AT ALL.

HOT DOUGHNUTS FOR BREAKFAST.

HEAT 1 CUP OIL IN
A SMALL FRY PAN OR
A SAUCEPAN

AND ONE TEASPOONFUL AT
A TIME SLIDE (THAT'S WHAT
THE SECOND SPOON'S FOR)
THE BATTER INTO THE OIL.
FRY MEDIUM BROWN

TAKE THEM OUT WITH A
FORK, AS THEY COOK.
SPRINKLE WITH SUGAR
AND RUSH (FASTER THAN
A SPEEDING BULLET) THEM
TO YOUR BEST BELOVED.

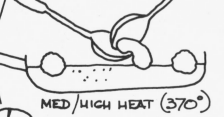

MED/HIGH HEAT (370°)

TURN THEM
TWICE & GIVE
THEM ROOM. THEY
PUFF UP.

WITH COFFEE OR CHAMPAGNE,
FLOWERS, CANDLES, LOVE
AND KISSES

Faggots

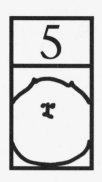

There are people who would have you call these Faggots *Frikadellen*, or even *Kuzu Ciger Colmasi*, and have you scurrying allover town looking for a copper pan exactly 2.75 centimetres deep. Faggots are basic working class food the world over, and in England, particularly in the north, they preceded the most famous of British folk foods, fish and chips.

Faggots and chips – we used to get them after a movie. There are still not as many cars in England as in North America, and making out in the back seat is the exception rather than the rule. After a movie in such outposts of the Empire as Nottingham, one announced the seriousness of one's intentions by suggesting first: "Wanna walk a bit?" and second: "'Ow about some faggots?"

There were those who took their newspaper-wrapped packets unashamedly to the river bank, but another school firmly convinced that horizontal sex was not nice repaired to dark shop doorways where they would consume their Faggots and chips over one another's shoulders...

Standing up, sitting down, off a plate or out of a newspaper, at cocktail parties or kid's dinners, they are simple, cheap, and I've never met anybody who didn't like them.

Chicken and Watermelon

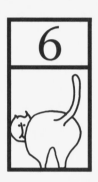

6

There comes a time when sitting on the porch spitting watermelon seeds interferes with serious conversation. Besides, the seeds pile up after a while; the mailman slips on them, and muggers use them for ammunition. But what to do? Every year watermelons get bigger and cheaper; every year the season gets longer.

Four of us, faced with an 18-pound monster, decided to take our solutions past the making of watermelon ice cream, beyond watermelon frappé and simple watermelon juice (all of them excellent but still undeniably watermelon). Fried watermelon just doesn't work very well, and the zucchini loaf freaks, carrot cake fiends and potato bread purists all draw the line at incorporating watermelon into their recipes.

Finally, as frequently happens after the second bottle of wine is opened, the obvious became obvious. Since chicken and watermelon usually come home in the same shopping bag, why not examine their potential for co-existence.

Chicken and watermelon has a fragile, evasive, delicate taste. It's easy to prepare, very pleasant on the palate, and uniquely North American.

A little rice with it is nice, maybe a couple of fried bananas dusted with cinnamon, or a handful of chopped roasted peanuts. But no matter how you serve it, you have every reason to look smug.

CHICKEN
AND
WATERMELON

CHICKEN
AND
WATERMELON

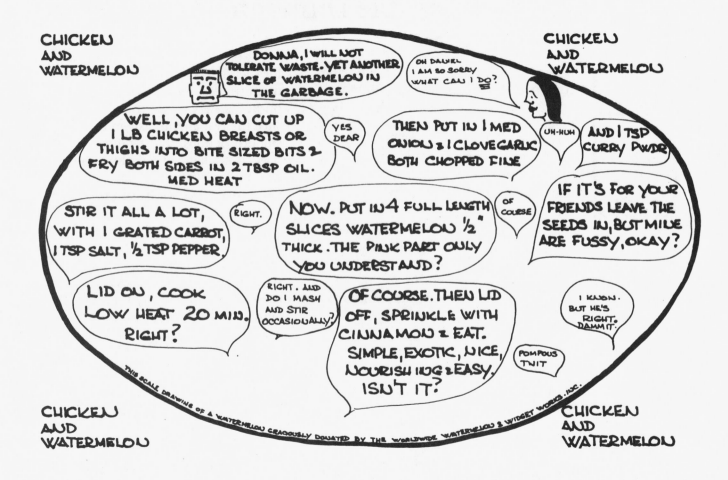

CHICKEN
AND
WATERMELON

CHICKEN
AND
WATERMELON

A Good Sensible Dinner for Four

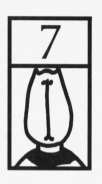

If you have the kind of in-laws who are convinced that their favourite child was temporarily insane when you set up house together, and that you yourself are permanently insane, totally incompetent and a burden to be endured, this is a good dish to have simmering on the back burner of your mind.

At first glance it looks suspiciously like trailer park food, but two things set it apart from those perfectly dreadful recipes the weekly newspapers run and re-run. The first is nutmeg, which redeems any ground beef recipe, the other is lettuce.

We always have lettuce around, getting a little tired in the fridge. But we very seldom think of cooking it. Keep some aside for the salad your in-laws usually insist upon (right after the obligatory comment on how pale your partner is looking) and slice the rest as thin as you can. It adds a smooth richness, quite different from cabbage. But whatever you do, don't stir it all about – let it remain in layers; and when you serve it, do not be surprised by their looking surprised. And pleased.

Besides, it takes so little time to prepare, and gives you forty minutes while it's cooking to kick a few socks under the chesterfield, ask the cat to move out of the laundry basket, stuff your *Joy of Sex* under the bedclothes and practice up on the Determined Smile. Actually, if you've got that kind of in-laws, this dinner's too good for them.

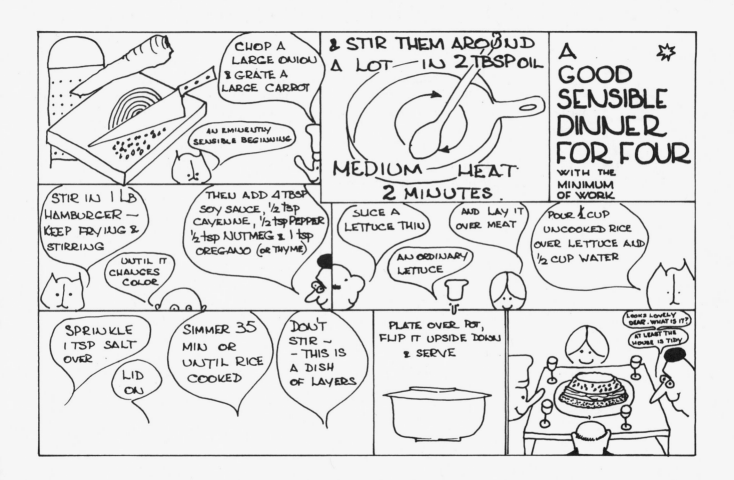

Spaghetti Without Meatballs

Agnolotti, bucatini, capellini, cappelletti – there are thousands of shapes and sizes of pasta, and hundreds of different ways of cooking each one. But nobody in North America seems to know that, so we settle for lasagna, spaghetti and meatballs, or, for the truly adventurous, spaghetti with clam sauce.

Time to try something else. You don't have to have meat, and once you get used to the idea of making a quick sauce – just a frypan and a little oil with whatever's at hand – you're half way to becoming really Italian.

And then you can think of uncooked sauces. Around Naples they chop fresh tomatoes, some garlic, a little basil, and marinate it all in a quarter cup of olive oil (and of course the tomato juices). If they haven't got basil they use oregano, and so can you. Thyme is okay, too, or marjoram. Marinating means letting everything sit – a couple of hours or all day while you're at work. Come home, cook the pasta, drain it, dump the tomatoes and oil on, toss it all and eat immediately.

Don't ever cook pasta before guests come; it's worth making them wait. And if you've got any pasta left over, toss it with a little olive oil, a little lemon juice and perhaps half a teaspoon of salt. A bit of finely chopped onion, some parsley, and next day (after it sits in the fridge all night) you've got a wonderful cold salad.

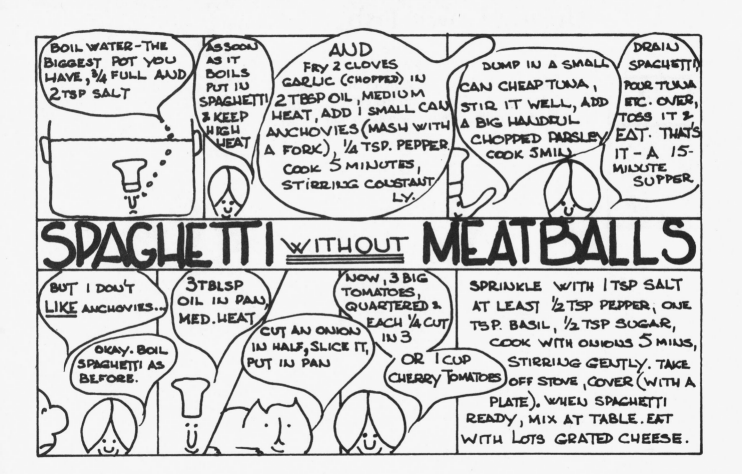

Upside Down Fish

A simple, honest, easy dish which tastes great. If we used a little cream instead of milk, and we called it *Filets de poisson à la façon de ma tante...*

Chicken and Dumplings

There comes a time, usually in the winter, when the cat is lost, your lover has gone, the car won't start and the buses are on strike, the cheque didn't come, the lab tests were positive ("but not to worry," said the doctor, "come in on Monday"), the plumbing is blocked and the landlord won't fix it, and life looks and sounds like an afternoon soap on black-and-white TV. This is when we need the classic *Saturday Evening Post* grandmother. We need freckles on our faces and a long drive out to the farm and most of all – sharp, sophisticated and city-slick as we may be – we need a cuddle.

You can go out and buy Mother Somebody's Homestyle Dinner, but it won't taste half as good as this, you won't get any pleasure out of making it, and nobody gives rave reviews to a packet. Just remember; always check the baking powder. Drop half a teaspoon in a little water. If it doesn't fizz, get some fresh.

There's nothing nicer than hearing your stomach say: "There, there, dear, everything's going to be fine." So dry your eyes, drink your milk, and don't eat all those cookies; you'll spoil your dinner...

Bubble and Squeak

British children learn at their mothers' knees to cook cabbage. Not just to cook it, but to destroy it – to give it a terrible reputation and make an international joke of it. But out of this soggy, tasteless mess they also learn to make a most magnificent dish called Bubble and Squeak, which when properly made is as close as the British will ever come to Soul Food.

To make an authentic Bubble and Squeak requires lamb left over from the Sunday roast and cold cooked potatoes from the same meal. Also quantities of leftover cooked cabbage, and that it be Monday, and that it be cooked by a Mum.

You won't find Bubble and Squeak in pubs because it's not a dish that lends itself to mass production. It's a dish I remember fondly from my childhood, and for years I knocked on the doors of British expatriates (always on Mondays) hoping that they would say apologetically, "There's only Bubble and Squeak"… but it seems to be a lower-class dish and therefore shameful – the sort of thing people eat in private.

So we had to develop a recipe for ourselves, using ingredients more readily available. This one tastes remarkably like the original: crusty on the outside, squishy in the middle. We frequently cook it on the boat where space, ingredients and time are always at a minimum.

Fagioli Toscanelli con Tonno

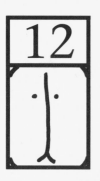

The big love of my life sat on a stool in a bookstore. She looked like a missionary who had decided to become a librarian, and she weighed 92 pounds. She drank like a fish, quoted Immanuel Kant and lived on a steady diet of cinnamon buns. Her refrigerator was full of mould and her kitchen cupboards were stacked from top to bottom with books. There was nothing to eat in her apartment.

I've since discovered that she is not unique. Children leaving home obviously can't carry a set of dishes, a spice rack and a set of copper cooking pots because, apart from anything else, that kind of junk spoils the image. But perhaps a bag of dried beans...

They don't have to be soaked overnight. They don't have to be fussed over. Beans are easy, and once you've accepted that they have an existence completely separate from tomato sauce and miniscule lumps of pork, and that canned beans taste like mush, you are three-quarters on the way to being successfully poor.

Let's not go into the nutritionists' spiel, or the stories about Mexicans living on beans and rice. Let's be a little more basic: beans taste good, they're cheap, and they are good for you. If you don't soak them overnight you can also forget about their musical effect. Don't ask me why, just experiment for yourself. Get a group of friends together. You could even write a thesis. Be my guest. And next time you're in the market, pick up some beans.

Easy Currant Cake

No fancy frosting, no oven and just one bowl to wash. Sunday afternoon tea when it's winter outside. A little jam is pretty good with this cake, or butter, but it can stand alone without anything else at all. We make it on the boat, but there's nothing against whipping it up in a ski-cabin, or in a plain ordinary kitchen in downtown anywhere.

Vegetables with Dignity, Style and Anchovies

There are no leftovers, ever.

Chicken and Oranges

15

Honest, simple, colourful, light, nourishing, different, easy, quick.

There was a time when I chose to believe that first-class passengers on airplanes actually had a little kitchen up front, with a French chef, a row of copper pots, and tanks full of live lobsters. Then one day I flew first class. We got free booze and food that was different from the proletariat's back there in tourist, or coach, or whatever they were calling the uncomfortable seats that year. But it wasn't any better.

This is a refinement of that day's *Poulet à l'Orange*. It's simpler and much better. If you want to fancy it up, add a little sherry with the orange juice, or grate a little fresh ginger into the pan at the start. Silver plates, paper ones or fingers, this is a very nice dish indeed. Use breasts the first time you try a new chicken dish; switch to thighs, which are cheaper but taste better. But remember you'll need your sharpest knife to bone them.

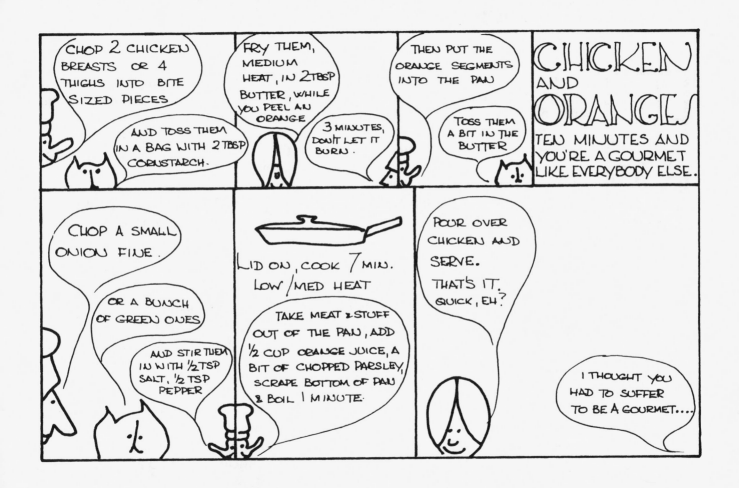

Cevapcici

16

There is an art to riding a donkey. A fast one travels at something less than two miles per hour if it's pointed towards home, and about half that in any other direction. A donkey is uncomfortable, uncooperative and unpredictable. Occasionally it will bite. And about three p.m. it starts looking for a place to spend the night. There is nothing you can do about it; it moves off the road and heads for any house that has a barn, and hay in the barn.

In Yugoslavia, where I first discovered donkeys, houses with barns seemed to anticipate donkeys and the people on their backs. There was always hay, and there was almost always lamb, usually a whole lamb cooking over an open fire, with a very old lady slowly turning it, basting it with oil, and sipping almost as regularly on a bottle of slivovitz.

Onion salad came with it: thin sliced raw onion with a little pepper, salt and pumpkin seed oil. Bread, of course, and red wine. It seemed to straighten you out, put the spark back in your eyes. There was always an hour or two to wait for supper, and if you were lucky, before the lamb, there would be Cevapcici (che-vap-chi-chi, if you're still wondering).

In the mountains outside Sarajevo they make Cevapcici from ground lamb. In the cities they sell them barbecued, without sauce, just chopped onions. And from house to house, like all good food, the recipe is different. This is the best we can do with what's regularly available to us, using local stuff. It's an enormous improvement on plain hamburger.

Of course if you've got a donkey, and a lamb or two, then all you need for total authenticity is an aged grandmother...

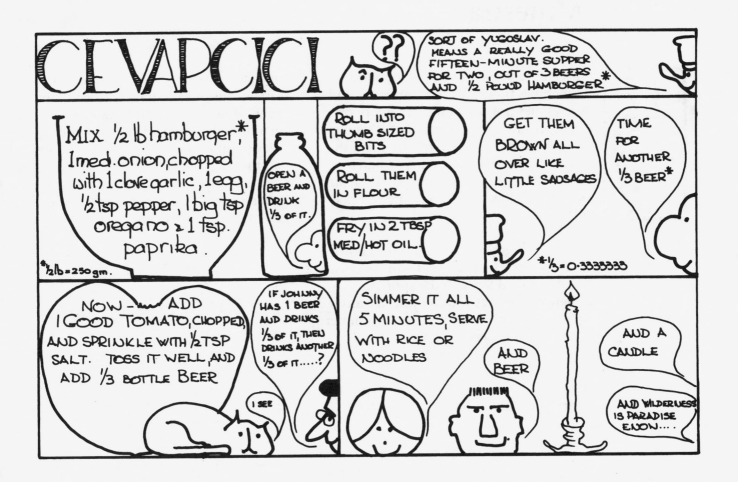

Minestra

It seems to vary from north to south; sometimes there's meat in minestra, and sometimes not. This one, a memory of Sicily, is strictly vegetarian, but it's a big, hearty, filling soup nevertheless, and the secret seems to be two kinds of starch. Here we're using beans and potatoes, but it works just as well with beans and rice, or potatoes and pasta.

We used to get through enormous bowls of it with the first bottle of wine because we discovered Sicily in the springtime, where rain makes you wet just like anywhere else, and if you have only summer clothes you get cold like anywhere else. We were sleeping cheap, which meant one toilet for twenty rooms, no bath, only cold water in the sink, and one blanket worn very thin.

Newspapers between the sheet and the blankets rustle a bit, but they warm you at night. Minestra warmed us in the evenings, no matter where we went, big cities or little villages; somebody always had the soup pot on. A good piece of cheese and some fruit make an authentic Italian dessert, and you can spend the money you save on wine.

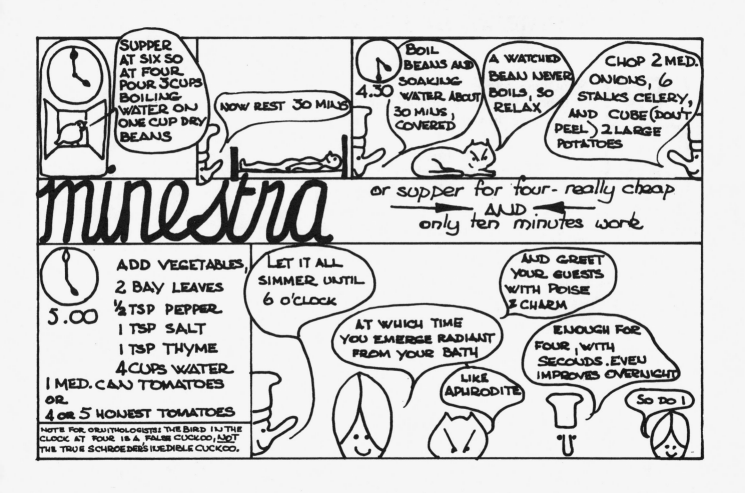

Corner Store Chowder

Sometimes you get stuck. Frozen fish, and somebody you like is coming. Someone who believes in you. Who needs a cuddle.

We call it born-again frozen fish. Of course it's much better with fresh, but it's pretty damn good just like this. And it's quick. Maybe twenty minutes. And it takes months to get an appointment with a shrink…

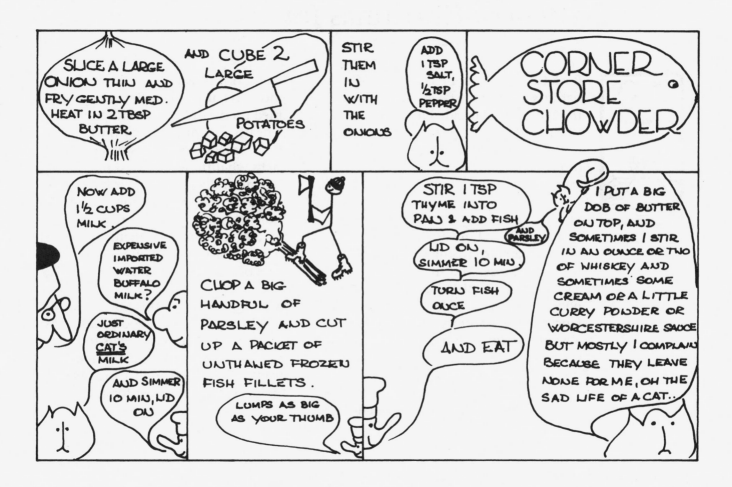

One-Pot Christmas for Two

19

Rock Cornish game hens are one of nature's drearier mistakes. Almost as though she had decided to make it all up to chickens for being so stupid and asked a television studio to dream up a glamorous, pocket-sized image for them to aspire to.

I've got nothing against Gidget, except that she's dull, dim-witted and sexless, a victim of an advertising department's puffed up prose. And that's what I've got against Rock Cornish game hens – they pop up in all sorts of fancy (and not so fancy) places, accompanied by unbelievable prose: "Pit bred fighting bantams at the peak of condition, oven-roasted in their own succulent juices and served at your table with our fabulous French Fries fried (in France) in a French French-fryer…"

Rock Cornish game hens have no natural juices. What you usually end up with is a dried up dwarf bird cowering in shame beneath a varnish of brown wallpaper paste. Small frozen birds (it sounds sad but that's what these are) need moist cooking (like most ducks) and their juices need supplementing with onions and garlic and more fragrant spices. There should be enough juice in the tomato and onion to make a sauce, but if you want to put in a glass of red wine, go ahead.

What comes out of this pot is a joy and delight, a particularly good Christmas dish; one bird apiece, fingers to lick, no oven to clean, no fuss, and a good smell everywhere. Two-people Christmases are the ones you remember for a long time.

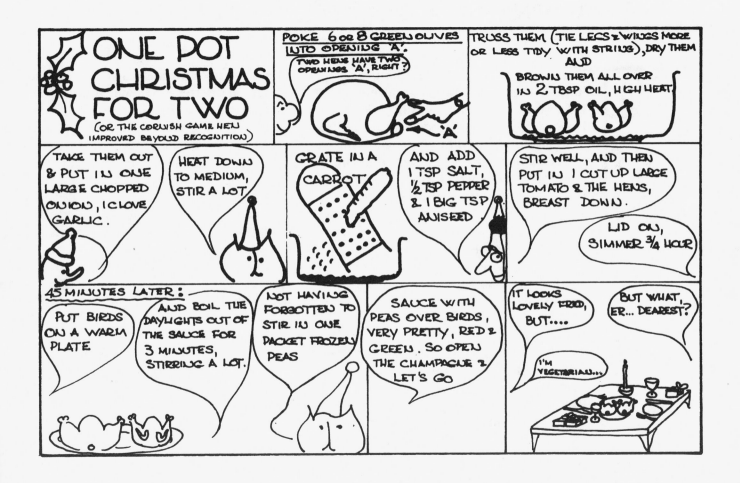

Chelo

Dried apricots are great for hiking snacks, lunch boxes, boat food and as candy for kids. I used to get bad looks from kids at Halloween when I offered them a handful of dried fruit instead of bubblegum, but as the years went by there appeared a hard core of kids who actually asked for fruit, which I thought was a triumph of common sense and proof of some nutritional instinct. Until I discovered that a local wheeler-dealer, aged ten, was trading in dried fruit, giving vast quantities of cheap candy for it, then selling it to his mother to make jam.

All over the world where fruit grows, people use dried fruit for cooking. In India, in Morocco, in Russia, in Persia – wherever people are poor, they dry such things as apricots because they don't have deep freezes, and then use them in the middle of winter to make a little meat go a long way.

Chelo is a poor people's dish. It keeps well (in fact, it's better next day), you can eat it with anything plain, like rice or pasta or pitta bread, and you can fancy it up as much as your palate or level of society demands, with roasted almonds or with mint chopped into the yogurt, and serve it with good wine or mint tea. And if you are a midnight snacker, it is wonderful cold, just spooned out of the dish and reflected upon. Somehow it doesn't work well with beef, but if you want to use chicken instead of lamb you won't be disappointed.

Let me show you — fry 2 lbs lamb stew in 2 tbsp oil. Cut it in cubes first, high heat, turn it a lot. About 2 minutes.

Wanna go bowling?

Turn heat down to medium and add 12 or 16 dried apricots, 1 clove chopped garlic, 1 big carrot (grated) 1 tsp cinnamon & ½ cup water.

That's it?

Almost. 1 tsp salt, ½ tsp pepper and simmer 2 hrs. Lid on, low heat. That's it.

So what do we do for 2 hours?

Bed....?

?

The T.V.'s up there....

Okay. We can watch the bowling.

CHELO

?

Just lamb and apricots, dear. All good things have fancy names. Don't worry. It's simple

NOTICE TO SOCIALLY PROMINENT PERSONS.

CHELO eats best sprinkled with fresh lemon juice at the table. Do you cut up the lemons in advance or let your British guests do it themselves? Decide, before your reputation is ruined.

2 HOURS LATER ~

I'll just quick fry a handful of almonds in 1 tbsp oil, medium heat, tossing them until they're golden.

And I'll mix 1 tsp mint into the meat

And I'll take the nuts quick out of the pan so Fred can chop them

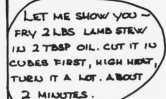

She put it all on the table, the lamb and the nuts and a dish of plain yoghurt & the lemons. And that very minute the door knob rang. It was a very important person who told them they had been selected to buy shares in the Brooklyn Bridge.

"We may be bowlers", said Fred (who was sharp) "but we're not stupid". The man sat down anyway (Chelo being that kind of dish) and saw the error of his ways. He now sells encyclopedias. Fred and Simma are famous for their Chelo parties. So there

The Best Carrot Cake in the World

Little Josiah Carrot was left an orphan at the age of six. Mailed by his parents to an aunt in Chicago, he was stamped "Insufficient Postage" and "Return to sender." His innocent holiday became a nightmare when the Post Office, relentlessly logical, decided that not only was postage insufficient to deliver him to Chicago but also totally inadequate to get him back to Sender. He was therefore consigned to limbo, where he shared a mail-bag with four other orphans and a dog named Ruff. All parcels, lost letters, orphans, bad cheque artists, dope smokers and persons having more than three unpaid parking tickets were eventually pardoned, given bus fare out of town and this carrot cake recipe.

The Copasetic Carrot Cake Co. Inc. was bankrupted by the 1978 crash in carrot futures. I met Josiah panhandling on a cold December day in New York. He told me the story of his life and finally sold me the recipe for ten dollars. If I had had more, no doubt I would have paid more.

Just check your baking powder before starting – drop a little in a glass of warm water and if it doesn't fizz, it won't work – stir a lot, and make sure you know what your astrological sign is, because carrot cake seems to bring that kind of thing out in people.

Me, I'm Aries, but my moon is in the back of a '52 Chevy.

Two More Vegetables

22

Get a little organized. Put the egg in one bowl and the bread crumbs in another alongside. Pick up a zucchini stick with one hand and slide it into the egg, but don't touch the egg. With the other hand twirl the zucchini around in the egg, transfer it to the breadcrumbs, and then roll it over to the edge of the plate. Pick up another zucchini with the first hand and repeat the process. That way you always have one hand clean and you aren't continually wiping your fingers on your apron. You can then pick up the breaded zucchini sticks with your clean hand and slide them into the pan. A very tidy operation, and very quick, once you get the hang of it.

The biggest problem with these zucchini is keeping up with the demand. Don't try to keep them wrapped in a towel in the oven; they're meant to be eaten immediately.

The cauliflower is extraordinary. Don't overcook it and don't forget the nutmeg. It's a very good dish to keep somebody busy with when you're running a friendly dinner party. There is nothing like the smile on a person's face when you deliver them from incompetence. They've never been able to cook, they were never shown how, they'd love to but they always screw up, right? And seven minutes later, total strangers are complimenting them. Makes you feel right proud.

Korma

Very bright, very colourful, and of course very easy. Most of the cooking happens while you're doing something else, so that life doesn't have to come to a grinding halt just because you've got people coming to supper.

Basically this is a Parsee dish, and the Parsees eat the best food in India, largely because they have absolutely no hang-ups and no religious prohibitions. If you're Jewish, they won't serve pork, if you're Hindu then there'll be no beef on the menu. Everything they cook is infinitely adaptable because food is first and foremost a social occasion.

Korma is a curry, but it's not intended to be a biker's special or an alternative to Drano. It will not make your hair fall out or smoke come out of your ears. It's mild and gentle and rich. And foolproof.

Har Tu Fay Kit

Bachelors traditionally eat out of the frypan. This recipe is just one step farther down the road to civilization. One frypan, one plate and two forks. We do it on the boat when it's raining and we're tired; then we put the dishes out on deck and let the rain wash them overnight.

Of course it's not really authentic Chinese food, but for that matter, what is? You can funk it up as much as you like – a little oyster sauce maybe, watercress instead of spinach, ground pork instead of beef, or, if you've got money, shrimp.

Once you learn the technique (which is basically getting the confidence to flip the pan over) you can try it with all sorts of other dishes. Use mitts or pot holders, because, naturally, the pan is hot. Hold tight and flip the pan quickly. Practice with an empty, cold pan first; that's the easy way to learn.

Meanwhile, cook this one with aplomb, and unless you have Madame Mao coming to dinner, nobody will call you on it. It's a change from the universal stir-fried vegetables, and it's the quickest made dinner I know.

Bannock

25

Hollywood used to insist that the West was won with the Colt.45 and the rather convenient habit the Bad Guys had of always wearing black Stetsons, which enabled the Good Guys, who were none too bright, to recognize them and hit them over the head with a chair.

But I became convinced at an early age that the real key to survival in cowboy country was bannock, the legendary bread that camp cooks made in th' embers of a dyin' fire, and the cowpokes wolfed down with their dawn coffee. Every Grade B Western I saw had bannock in it some- where; so did the Western magazines, and so did all the outdoor cookbooks. For years I tried to make it. I followed all the instructions, I bought hand-milled flour, and once I even carried water from the "crick" in m' cowboy hat. But nothin' worked. All I got were sodden lumps with a burned outside, too heavy for a Frisbee and too hard for a cushion.

I figgered that the Code of the West, which came out strong against all sorts of dishonourable behaviour, didn't extend to lyin' about campfire bread. So instead of ridin' off into the sunset, I went Bad and took to kissin' Miss Emmy, even stayin' overnight.

The League of Cowboys for the Code couldn't, by their constitution, gun me down, and I never go into bars that have chairs, so they finally came up with this here recipe, and asked me to mend my ways.

It works. The hole is the secret because it lets the heat into the previously soggy middle. It's crusty, it's wonderful with butter, and the only problem is that Miss Emmy likes it so much she reckons I ought to stay every night.

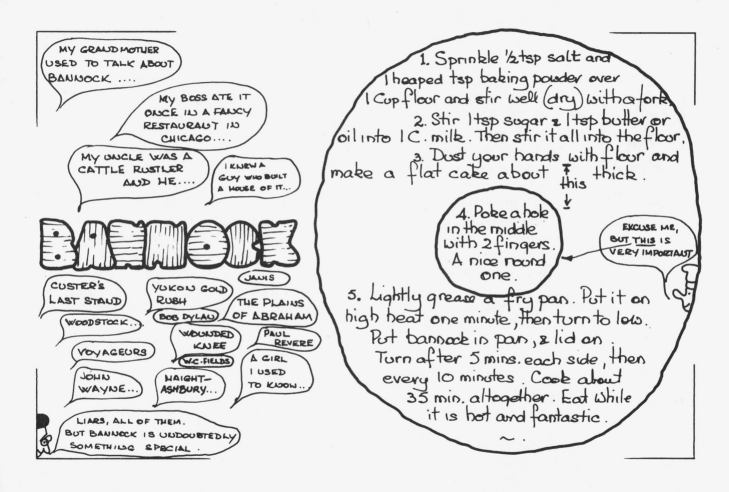

Tijuana Barbecue

Half an hour's drive from San Diego (just over ten minutes if you're a California driver), is the Mexican border. And the border is Tijuana, a city of 24-hour-a-day nightclubs, of fresh-pressed fruit juices sold on the street, of poverty and wealth, of little kids with more financial acumen than a Montreal furrier, of cheap tequila, good beer, wonderful food and, despite the popular myth, a lot of hardworking people. They work hard because they're poor and don't want to stay that way.

They like to eat, but they don't have a lot of time to cook. They don't have a lot of fancy equipment either, and they buy cheap meat because it's cheap. People go to Tijuana from Los Angeles and San Diego, and they bring back, or try to bring back, all sorts of exotic goodies.

I bring back peppers, fifteen or twenty different varieties – mild ones, musty ones, purple ones, red hot screamers, yellow ones – and they all have different uses. I also bring back memories of magnificent, cheap and flavourful meals, and spend months trying to duplicate them with what's available in my corner store.

This recipe is an adaptation of a lady called Beth's adaptation of her memory. It tastes remarkably authentic, and it's a real reputation-maker for a very little money. Cook it very, very slowly: go out to a movie, go shopping, do the laundry, just don't worry about it. The meat fibres will separate, so you can pull it apart with a fork and shovel it onto bread or tortillas. Warm it up next day with a little extra wine or water. Always cook it slowly, lick your fingers frequently and for best effect use no plates – just tortillas and a deft hand.

Chicken and Peanuts

The most difficult part of making this dish is preventing your guests from eating the ingredients. So hide the peanuts until you're ready to cook, then do it quicker than a three-card monte hustler. After you have made this dish with chicken breasts, move on to the cheaper parts like thighs and legs (by this time you'll think nothing of cutting the bones out), and finally start to buy whole chickens and make soup and stock with the back and wings.

How to make stock? A big pot, all the bits of chicken you don't use, an onion cut up and a carrot. Cover with water, bring to a boil, skim the froth off after 15 minutes (it's easy with a spoon – you don't *have* to have a skimmer), turn the heat down as low as it will go and let it simmer, lid on, all night, or at least while you go to a movie. Strain the stock into a jar, keep it in the fridge and use it to cook with; or add a few chopped vegetables and a little salt and pepper for instant soup.

Make this dish first with peanuts. Then try almonds, or cashews, even walnuts. Coconuts are not recommended unless you're cooking an ostrich.

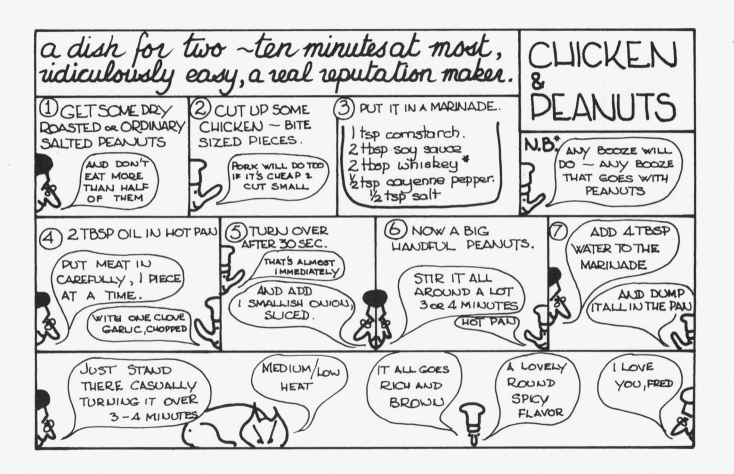

Leek and Potato Soup

28

This is really where this book started. It was November and raining and Sunday and sad. There were three of us in a cottage. Pictures of the cottage in summer showed roses round the door, thatch on the roof and an unmistakable air of English countryside curling over the picket fence. The reality of it in winter was mud to the doorstep, damp from floor to ceiling, no electricity, mice in the walls and the only form of heat a fireplace that smoked into the house instead of out.

We made this soup without leeks from onions we found in a shed. We had half a garlic sausage left over from Saturday's picnic, and there were potatoes with the onions. It was wonderful. Tiredness and hunger will always spice up the plainest dish.

You can make this soup from almost anything. Leeks are nice but not absolutely necessary. A bit of leftover ham works instead of bacon, and if you don't put in any meat at all but add a half-cup of cream two minutes before serving, it's still delicious. Put it through a blender and chill it for vichyssoise; or mash it a bit with a wooden spoon (the way I like it, just a little lumpy) and it has a simple home-made innocence about it.

The essential ingredient is the nutmeg, which mice don't appear to like. I'm not suggesting nutmeg as a mouse repellent, but I am insisting on it for this soup or any variations of it. Nutmeg is a great spice to have around; it transforms the dullness of cauliflower, it makes rice pudding attractive even to five-year-olds, and of course it is basic to hot winter drinks. Try a bit sprinkled on warmed (not boiled) beer, with a little lemon juice added and a spoonful of sugar. Sensational.

Eight-Legged Chicken

29

You have to prepare this early, before the guests arrive. Don't drink too much while you're doing it or it will look like a low budget horror movie; and try to get someone to help you, because a secret shared is containable. People think you're crazy if you walk around alone for an hour before dinner smiling that secret smirk, but if there are two of you smiling they just think you're overreacting to sex in the afternoon.

I don't overstuff chickens because they take so much longer to cook. I just poke a few bits of something nice inside their back door – some chopped lemons and a handful of garlic, or some chopped onions and a teaspoonful of thyme. Or some chopped apples. Or just lemon juice and tarragon. I rub them well with salt (makes the skin crisp), I use a 400°F oven, and I baste them every fifteen minutes with butter. This chicken goes brown all over, and if you don't have too many lights on (candles are best) people can't see the stitches. When they stop laughing you just snip the thread and suddenly everybody's got supper. It doesn't work with a turkey, but it will with a capon, and there it is, an unforgettable dinner for ten.

When you get really skillful at the stitching, next thing you know you'll be doing nose jobs for your friends.

Duck and Red Cabbage

30

I'm not entirely sure that the leftover soup isn't the best part of any dinner, particularly if the party people (in this case two of you) are still around. (It does happen that way. I have friends who met at a New Year's Eve bash, walked home with one another and never walked out again; they're still enjoying variations on the theme of their original party.)

Even if it doesn't turn out to be some enchanted evening, enjoy the duck and then clear the table. Shove all the leftovers, except cake or other sweet stuff, into your biggest saucepan: potatoes or noodles, rice, salad, bones, uneaten duck (or turkey, or chicken), vegetables, just *everything*. Bring to a boil, put the lid on and simmer – just forget about it – on the lowest heat, for two or three hours, even, if you're comfortable with simmering, overnight.

Let cool with the lid slightly ajar, skim off all the visible fat, pick out the biggest pieces of meat, and strain the rest. The juice may need a little salt, but what I do is add a lot of pepper and a tablespoon of vinegar for an instant hot and sour soup. Or you can put a big teaspoon of thyme in it, and some vegetables cut very thin and you've got an instant potage. Whatever you do to it, leftover soup can't go wrong; it has that legendary back-of-the-stove, French farmhouse quality that people rave about.

Some Cheaper and Easier Alternatives to Cake

Desserts tyrannize most social meals.

People work their butts off to make something unusual and wonderful for supper; they shop and cook and worry and spoil their sex lives for days ahead, and before their guests are halfway through the soup they're speculating on what the dessert will be, talking about a wonderful cake that Valerie made, and refusing second helpings "so I'll have room for dessert."

It seems almost obligatory to make something rich and creamy, indigestible and fattening. I prefer the desserts of Italy, where fruit is slowly and elegantly peeled and savoured, but occasionally I muck about with my fruit, make pretties of it, and serve very small portions. These three suggestions will in no way reduce your reputation, and you won't have to sit there fuming while some oaf (usually the one who smokes between courses) raves over a cake that two hours before was in the frozen foods section of the local market.

Besides, any leftovers are fine for breakfast, and no matter how depraved you might be, you can't eat cake at 7:00 a.m.

SOME ALTERNATIVES TO CAKE ~ CHEAPER & EASIER

PEEL AND QUARTER 1 PEAR FOR EACH TWO PEOPLE.

BOIL ¼ BOTTLE RED WINE WITH 3 SLICES FRESH GINGER, 4 CLOVES AND A SQUEEZE LEMON JUICE

NO FRESH GINGER USE POWDERED, NO CLOVES USE CINNAMON.

SIMMER PEARS 20 MIN., TAKE OUT, BOIL WINE FAST 2-3 MINS, POUR OVER PEARS.

THUS WE MAKE A SYRUP

EAT HOT OR COLD, WITHOUT WHIPPED CREAM

APPLES ~ ~ DESSERT OR BREAKFAST

OR BOTH

PEEL, QUARTER & SLICE THIN AN APPLE

PUT 3 TBSP PLAIN YOGHURT IN A BOWL

LAY APPLE PRETTILY, SQUEEZE LEMON JUICE

REGARDE, ZE APPLE 'OW PRETTY SHE LAY

DRIBBLE MAPLE SYRUP OVER, SPRINKLE SESAME SEEDS

THE ALMOST ALL-CANADIAN DESSERT

MEXICAN ORANGES

CUT UNPEELED JUICY ORANGES CROSSWISE INTO ¼" SLICES.

LAY THEM IN A NICE BOWL WITH 2 TBSP SUGAR (FOR EACH PERSON) SPRINKLED OVER.

POUR 1 OZ RUM (FOR EACH PERSON) OVER & LET SIT AN HOUR OR MORE. EAT WITH YOUR FINGERS.

RUM OR TEQUILA

THEY KILL FOR THE JUICE...

Coq au Bière

Perhaps it should be *Coq à la Bière*, but we're not being strictly French about this; we're making country food – a mellow, rich and simple dinner the likes of which I've enjoyed in France and Belgium and Holland, in Denmark and in Poland. Anywhere that people brew beer and eat chicken you'll find variations of this dish because that's the way real cooking develops – not from a complicated foreign recipe, but from whatever's at hand half an hour before dinner time.

Don't be miserly with the seasonings. Pepper and salt are always a matter of personal taste, but the thyme here is the essential: it gives a good robust country taste. Serve some honest bread, and if you want to stretch the beer a bit try cutting it, half-and-half, with ginger beer, which the British call a shandy. The easiest way to find ginger beer is to follow a Jamaican: they drink it at home and have an underground network for finding it elsewhere.

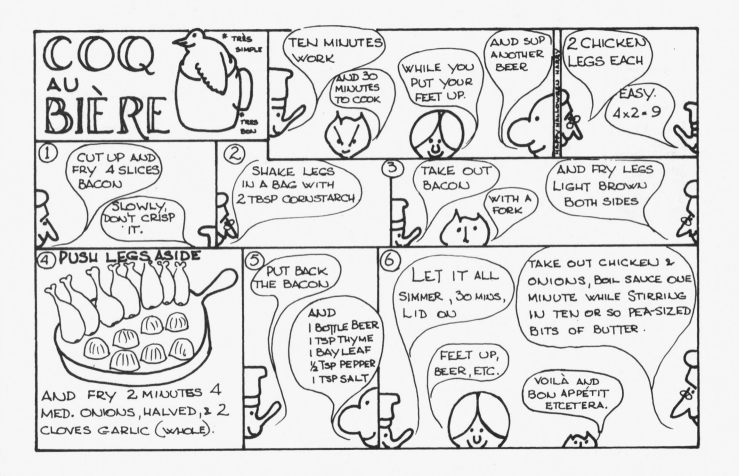

Chickpeas

Here is the cheapest protein you can buy. Cook your own and they'll have a crunch. If you insist on buying canned ones, drain them, rinse them well to get rid of the slimies, and serve them as if they were real food. Once you discover dried chickpeas (they're no trouble; just put them to soak in water before you go to bed or work) you'll discover all kinds of recipes because people will bring them to you as special gifts. Chickpea people have passwords and a secret handshake. There's a spring in their step, a confidence radiating from their smile. Could it be simply their inner works reacting to the extra protein they're getting? Or is it something more?

Let me tell you that my life has changed since I found chickpeas. And I want you right now to put your hand on this book and let it happen to you. I want you to abandon the earthly pleasures of peanuts and popcorn and come to chickpeas.

Take a bowlful to your next party and see how many converts you make. Like most religions, the central character goes under a variety of names. You might find chickpeas called garbanzos – or even ceci beans.

Stifado

34

Buy whole cloves because the powdered ones lose the oil, which makes the taste. One clove between the gum and an aching tooth will see you through until the dentist gets back from the golf course; two cloves transform even the most commonplace of curry powders; three in applesauce, the same in rhubarb; a few in stewed plums, in mulled wine, in hot beer drinks, in tea, in lemonade, in marinades; stuck in ham, of course; stuck in onions that are going into a stew (particularly good with oxtail), and in this very comforting Greek stew – Stifado.

And if you want to do something particularly nice for a Christmas present, buy a couple of jars of cloves and seek out the roundest, most perfect medium-size orange in the market. Poke a hole through the skin with a toothpick, then stick in a clove. And another and another, all the way round its waist in a straight line, as close as you can get them to one another. Another line above the first, one below, and so on, until the whole orange bristles with cloves. The Elizabethans called them pomanders and carried them about believing that the sweet aromas would protect them against infection. Nowadays people put them in their underwear drawer, and they're supposed to last as long as love is true. I once flew from Vancouver to New York to spend Christmas with my true love and spent the whole trip making her a pomander. The airplane was filled with a wonderful smell, and when I got to her apartment her roommate told me sorry but she'd gone to Puerto Rico with a computer programmer. The pomander didn't explode, so I gave it to the roommate. We had a good Christmas.

Three Perversions of Mushrooms

35

The gourmet stores are full of little packets of hideously expensive dried mushrooms imported from the gourmet capitals of the world. Like most dehydrated foods, when the moisture goes most of the flavour goes too, and the mushrooms become pale imitations of the fresh boletus or chanterelles that were originally picked in some Polish or Italian forest. Mushrooms are ninety per cent water – not just plain old tap water, but nice flavourful juice. And yet most cooked mushrooms have been fried so thoroughly that the juice has evaporated and they are chewy, tasteless and bland.

Supermarket mushrooms used to be cheap, but not any more. So we should stop treating them as incidentals, or as an accompaniment to steak, and we should give them back a little dignity. Most cookbooks will say, "Don't cook mushrooms in olive oil." Forget that advice and use the best olive oil you can afford – what the Italians call "Extra Virgin" – and be generous with it. (Fry a thick slice of good bread in a couple of tablespoonsful of olive oil, sprinkle on a little salt and pepper, and see for yourself what simple taste is all about.) Be generous with the herbs and keep the lid on most of the time. Don't overcook mushrooms, and don't be scared to buy the big brown ones because, after all, you don't want them to taste like those canned button mushrooms or you wouldn't be reading this book.

If you want to be truly perverse, stir in a couple of tablespoons of thick cream for the last three minutes of cooking.

THREE PERVERSIONS OF MUSHROOMS

FIRST, slice ½ lb mushrooms **thick** — stalks and all (at least a half inch). Set aside.

In 2 tbsp olive oil fry 1 clove chopped garlic for 1 minute. Now choose your perversion.

① Add sliced mushrooms to pan. Sprinkle ½ tsp salt, 1 tsp oregano. Toss well, lid on, cook 6 minutes. LOW HEAT

② Add mushrooms, add 2 tsp tomato paste & 2 tbsp water. ½ tsp salt, 1 tsp oregano. Mix well, cook 3 min. lid on, 3 min. lid off. Stir frequently.

③ Add 4 anchovy fillets to pan, mash smooth. Add 1 large tomato cut up, cook and squash down 1 minute. Heat to LOW. Add mushrooms, 1 tsp MINT, ½ tsp salt, ½ tsp pepper. Cook 3 min. lid on, 3 min. lid off. 2 people, a glass of wine, some fried bread — who needs more....

What's a perversion?

frequently something nice.

other what?

that other...

that other people don't yet know about...

Dinner in 20 Minutes If You Hurry, 25 If You Don't

36

Art was once a snob's private park. I used to be told that I couldn't paint or draw. I used to be taken to museums and shown what real art was, and most of the time I was too terrified to even try to understand what I was seeing.

Food used to be almost the same experience. It couldn't be fun, it had to be serious, and you had to know all the names, preferably in a foreign language.

Then I discovered that the French made food, and made love, in their own language. They cooked because they were hungry, and they made love because they were passionate. We had it all confused: if we weren't doing it with a French accent it was meaningless, and a whole race of gourmets squeezed itself into *la cuisine* and *l'amour*. If Charles Boyer had had an

American accent, he could never have said, "Come wiz me to ze Kasbah..."

If you let your gourmet friends get at this dish, they will call it *Poulet Bonne Femme*, which to the French means almost anything with potatoes, a bit of bacon and some peas in it. Traditionally they use salt pork if they've got it, and so can you. But while your high-class friends are desperately shopping all over town for snob ingredients, you and your simpler friends are sitting down to supper, getting into the second bottle of wine, and maybe commenting on the fact that eating is, first of all, fun.

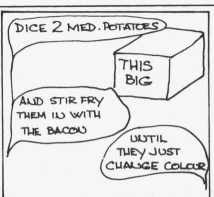

DINNER IN 20 MINUTES IF YOU HURRY ~ 25 IF YOU DON'T

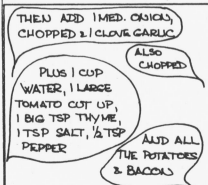

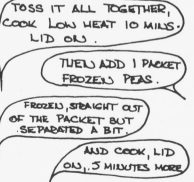

Chicken Liver Paté

In junk stores you can find cups, or little bowls, souvenirs of somebody's honeymoon, of trips to Disneyland or even, as my favourite mug proudly proclaims, "Presented by The Women's Credit Managers Breakfast Club for Perfect Attendance." There are honey pots, old mustard pots, marmalade jars, even odd wineglasses. If you don't insist on a set, or a matching saucer, you can pick them up for less than a dollar.

Then you can fill them with chicken liver paté, carefully pour butter over the top, tidy up any splashes, and have a perfectly acceptable Christmas present. If you want to make it bigger, wrap a box of crackers too, the whole tied up with ribbon.

This is the only recipe in the book that calls for special equipment. If you don't have a blender, mash the paté as smooth as you can with a fork – the butter will smooth it all out. And why no salt? Well, as all Jewish grandmothers know, salt makes the edges go dark. Sprinkle on a little salt when it's actually on the cracker.

Lady Di's Nanny's Fave Pudding

38

You can be a convicted dope dealer, a politician, a mugger of the elderly or a stealer of babies' rattles, a stockbroker, wiretapper, hangman, bank manager, even a baseball umpire – but if you can make a decent pudding, you're acceptable in any society. There's something so virtuous about pudding, something utterly whole-some. It's the good old days all over again with your stomach purring "thank you."

If you're ashamed of the simple virtues and insist on the sophistications of the gourmet set, put an ounce or two of booze in with the fruit, or a squirt or two of lemon juice. You can slice apples to go with the berries, or use jam thinned with water; you can pour cream over it all, or custard. And you can even not make a dessert at all but put leftover curry in the bottom of the pan with a little water, or leftover stew, dump the dough on top, and there it is: a meat pudding just waiting for a little salad to be a complete dinner.

You don't have to go to private school, or have a nanny, or be rich....

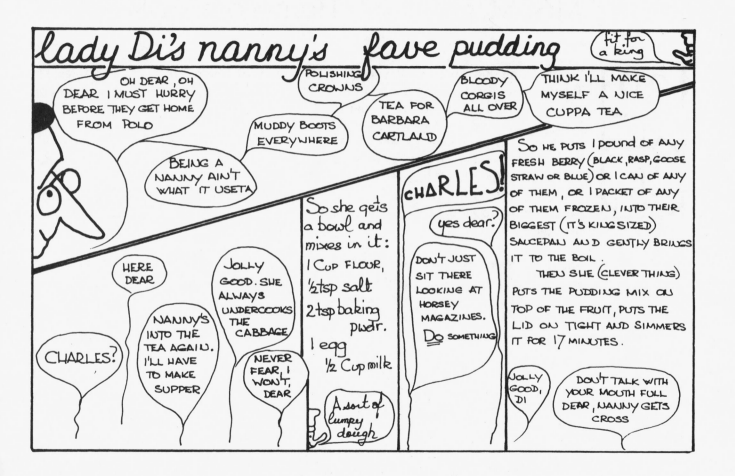

Mrs. Marco Polo's Homecoming Stew

"Marco," she said, "where have you been? Twenty-four years you're gone and I'm supposed to believe it was just a boat ride? I was *worried*. And this Chinese food story? I've seen it on the television, Marco, it doesn't take 24 years, it's *quick*. So where you been? What's her name? Can she cook? Whatsa matter, you don' like Mama's food no more? Eat, eat, mangiare, mangiare…"

The only difference between Jewish mothers and Italian mamas is that the Italian ones can be bought off cheaper. Mrs. Marco P. didn't need any more than a little soya sauce to divert her, maybe a little aniseed and the idea of using orange peel.

I first discovered this stew in Naples. She was a nice lady who had never heard of Chinese food, but somebody special must have handed it down to her, because the Chinese do almost exactly the same thing – orange peel, soya sauce and star anise.

Everybody knows about Marco Polo bringing home tomatoes and noodles to Italy, and then Catherine de Medici taking good food to France. But nobody seems to have thought of this Italian recipe that puts stew and stew together.

mrs marco polo's homecoming beef stew ~

~ take 1lb beef stew (cut up) and toss it in a bag with 3 tbsps flour.

~ fry it all sides, medium heat, in 2 tbs oil

~ add, all at once : ½ tsp pepper, 3 tbsp soya sauce, 1 tsp aniseed and 1 tsp mustard.

~ also 3 large tomatoes (or a can) and the peel of an orange.

~ simmer it one and a half hours, lid on

what do Italians do for 1½ hours? | sing? | change governments? | open a restaurant? | get tighter pants? | all wrong. Why you think there are so many Italians...?

Nouveau Quiche

40

Quiche is no big deal, despite its sudden rise to fame at blue-rinse brunches. It's usually dull, it's been frozen, frequently it was bought from some little gourmet supply shoppe, and at worst it came out of a package – just add water and stir. If you don't gush over it, you'll never get invited back again, which might not be such a bad thing after all, except that the people who are the worst offenders with quiches are usually those most able to afford something better.

Nevertheless, quiche has a certain chic, probably because of a folk memory locked away in an unused corner of your brain. It seems that every civilization known to man and Kenneth Clark has spent its formative years looking for an alternative to plain boiled eggs. The Spaniards make *tortilla*, the Italians call the same dish *frittata*, the Japanese steam eggs into *chawan mushi*, and North America swings between the short order cook's delight (a Denver omelet) and 27 varieties of quiche, most of which would make perfectly good sound absorbing pads for typewriters.

My alternative is basically an omelet, but because it is cooked slowly, and covered, it has a different texture, and the little bit of water in it makes it light. It's very good hot and equally good cold. It keeps, it packs to carry onto an airplane (the Anti-Rubber Chicken Movement grows stronger daily), and best of all it teaches you the flipping technique which once mastered will open the door to all kinds of recipes that once called for an oven.

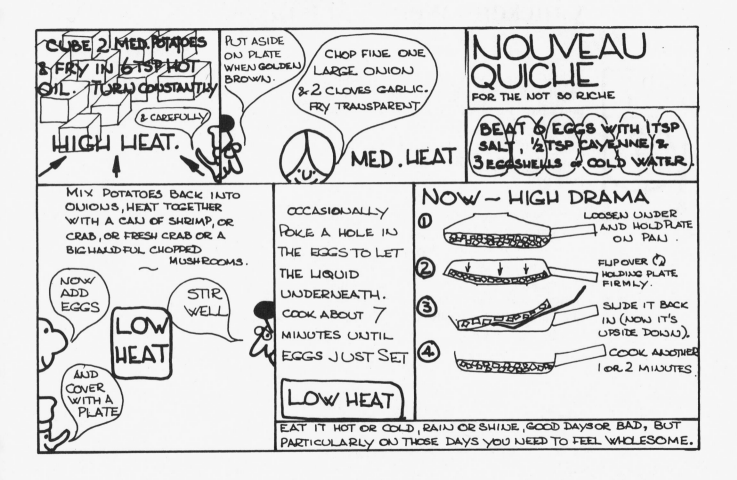

Chicken Livers and Grapes

In France they use duck livers and some very fancy booze called Armagnac. We don't have much of either, so I reworked this recipe into standard supermarket ingredients. Which of course is the only way to cook. Use what's handy, and do your best.

This is a ridiculously simple dish, which can stand up against anybody's pretensions of haute cuisine. It is quite wonderful when cherries are used instead of grapes, and if you want to be really imaginative you can whizz it through the blender, put it in little bowls, chill it for an hour or so and serve it as a mousse. All good things are simpler than we think.

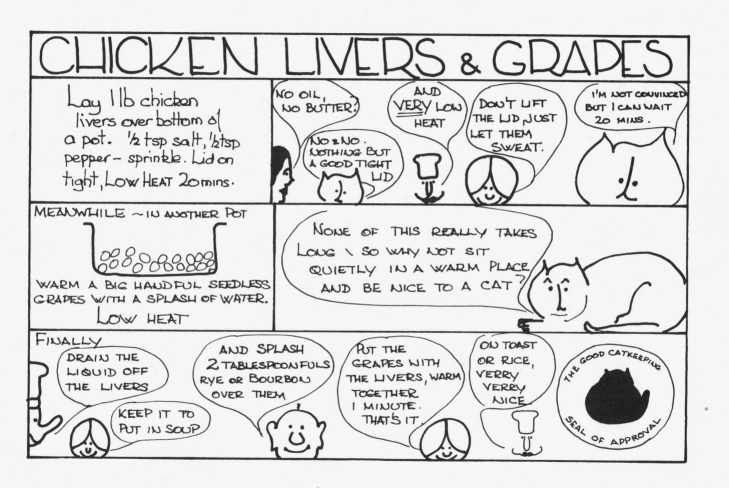

Chicken Wings Are Cheap

Dogs when very hungry will lick the fingers of people who have eaten fried chicken, but people, despite what the commercials say, are usually more interested in finding a paper towel to get the stuff off before they have to take their pants to the cleaners.

Real finger lickin' chicken is indeed rare, and it's not that popular. This recipe is certainly not for WASP cocktail parties, or indeed any party where white gloves are required. This chicken is sticky, messy and wonderful, and I like to go at it sitting around a table with a couple of good friends and a little Jack Daniels Black. But if you want to make these wings for a party, get everything ready beforehand and be prepared to stand at the stove making batches as fast as people eat them.

That's how you establish a reputation.

Some Special Spaghetti from Sicily

Sicily was to be a working breakthrough. I intended to spend two months writing this book – working afternoons. I had visions of a quiet shady bar, a bottle of wine at my elbow and a goat nuzzling my feet. Right after lunch I was going to start; two pages a day and the rest of the time lolling in the lap of the Mediterranean.

But there was a problem. Everybody in Sicily eats lunch. Around 12:30 they start, slowly with a bottle of wine. The local garage mechanic, the coffin maker, the baker, the local lawyer and his mistress, some fishermen – they all take off to a restaurant and they talk. They talk some and eat some, then talk some more and eat some more. Lunch seems to finish around 3:30, unless it's an important one, in which case it might go on until four.

Then it's time for a little rest somewhere behind closed shutters. The bars are not open, the stores are not open, and even the police are nowhere to be seen. There is nothing to do until around five, when the stores and bars open again for a couple of hours, just to fill in the time before dinner. Which is the big meal of the day. I didn't get any writing done. But I learned an awful lot about spaghetti, and never ate the same dish twice.

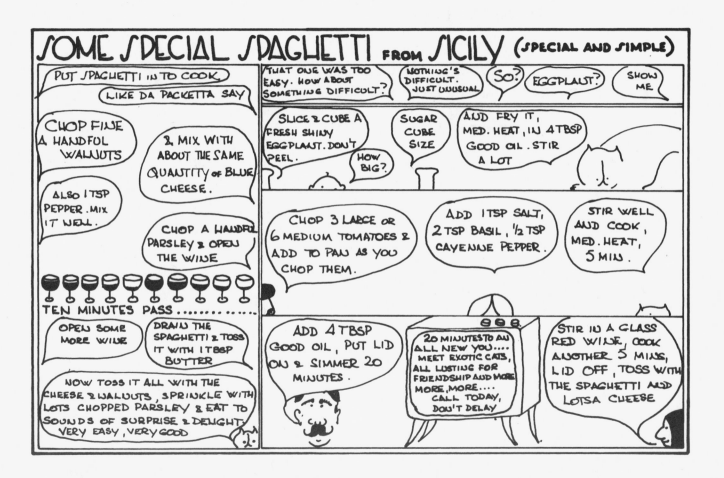

Chicken Tovarich

Wolves, beautiful women in horse-drawn sleighs, ice and snow everywhere, and potatoes and vodka. You know what Russia is like. A primitive version of North Dakota.

It was quite a shock to find that there are light, joyous, sunny dishes in Russian, food made with sun-warmed fruits, and as exciting as any Italian every imagined – all of them easy to make and most of them digestible, even without vodka.

I was shown this dish using pomegranate juice, which is hard to get. Red wine is a perfectly acceptable substitute; or you can use cranberry juice with an extra clove of garlic and a teaspoonful of vinegar, or plain grape juice with a little vinegar and some orange peel. Don't get bogged down in dogma; just enjoy this thick, dark red, flavourful dish. If you have sauce left over, keep it in a cup in the fridge and use it on spaghetti.

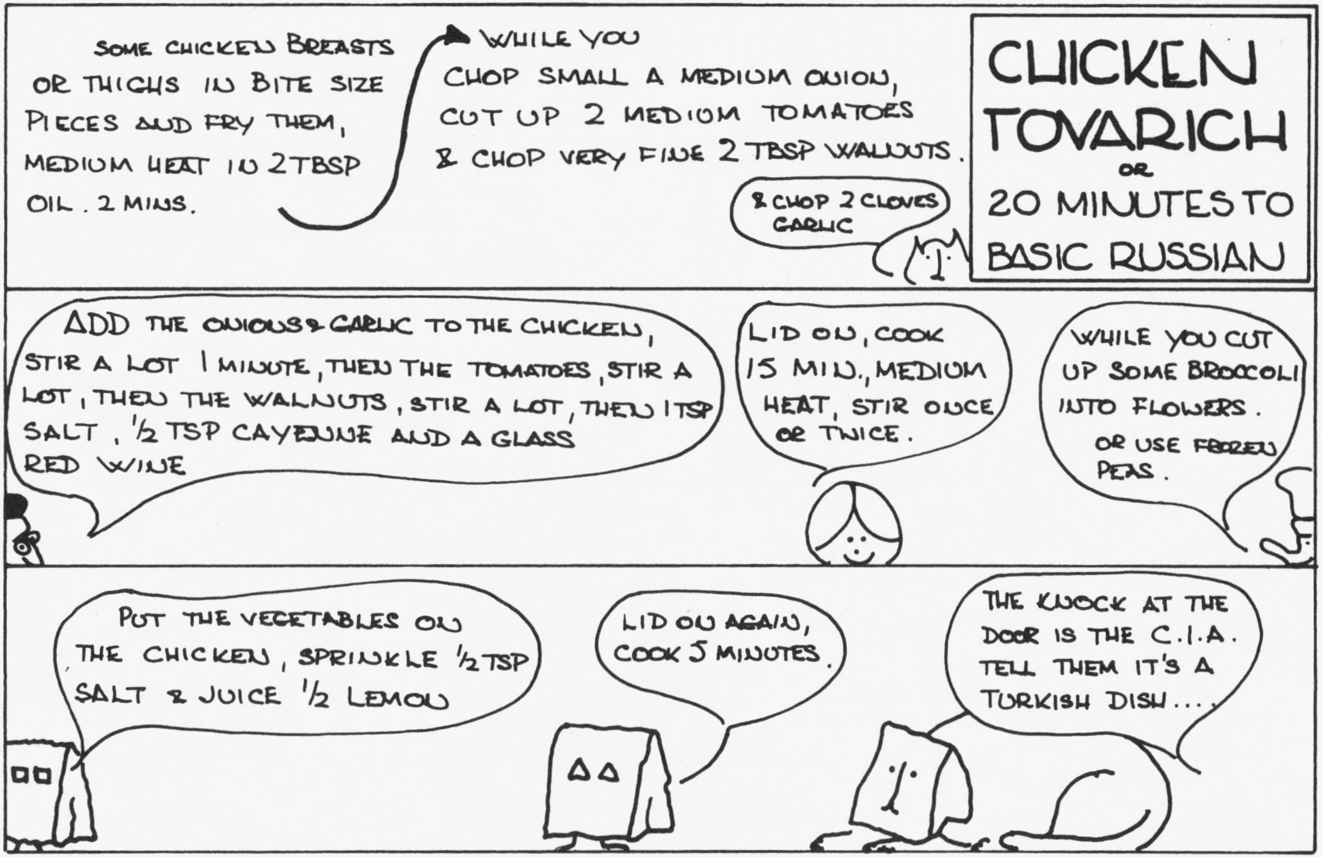

DO NOT ADMIT TO STRANGERS THAT YOU COOK RUSSIAN FOOD.

Index